With Love from Joy

CHANNELLED WORDS OF WISDOM

Moya Love

Copyright © Moya Love
First Published 2013

First print: Island Publishing.
P.O. Box 398 Mona Vale, NSW, 1660
With Love from Joy: Copyright © 2013

ISBN: 978-0-646-57548-3

Cover Design: 'Together Again' painted by Moya Love.
Typesetting: Linkletters – Perth, W.A.

Purchase through Amazon.com

National Library of Australia

Cataloguing in Publication data:

Love, Moya

With Love from Joy.

E: moyalove@outlook.com

Thank You

I WOULD like to express my sincere appreciation to all those who have supported me in the completion of this book.

Thank you to my daughter, Claudia Ferrante, for your continued encouragement, my personal computer guru, Sven Varendorff, and my friends who have read pages of my manuscript with interest.

To Andy and Tamara Cooke, thank you so much for your flattering photography and other assistance.

Sincere thanks to Sally Odgers and Elly Bradbury who edited my manuscript. I would also like to acknowledge Elizabeth Bezant, who coached and encouraged me at the beginning of this manuscript.

Thank you *Joy* for your trust in me.

My Story

Moya Love

MY GRANDMOTHER, Hannah, was the first person in Spirit to write to me. I had been sitting under a tree with pen and paper, trying to solve a problem by writing out my thoughts, when I started scribbling with an Irish lilt.

I became aware that I could hear her so I wrote out her whispers, and with her help, I was able to gain clarity on issues that were worrying me. This was the first of our many 'talks' on paper. Through this experience, I came to understand I was clairaudient and since that time I have become very familiar with my pen travelling across the page of its own accord as I have written for myself and on behalf of others from the Spirit World.

From the age of twelve my health had suffered due to Scheuermann's Disease. Consequently, I was prescribed daily pain-killer tablets and by the time I was in my mid-thirties they were doing more harm than good.

A friend recommended a healer, and I began seeing this lady on a regular basis. During this time I discovered I could reduce my pain and discomfort by adjusting my energy field to the healing light that she would channel to flow through me. My intention was to heal my physical body and in allowing myself to receive this loving energy, I was able to look into my emotional background and start the process of forgiving my past. This was the beginning of the understanding that the light that I was receiving would not only balance and repair the discs, nerves and muscles in my back, but also provide me with a secure environment in which to heal my emotional body.

I learnt that there was no limit to the healing grace I could attract. My way of doing this was to still myself in meditation and humbly ask the healing realms in the Universe to bring me the transformative gifts of grace and light and then direct this light to the areas that I wanted to balance and heal.

I discovered that changing old belief patterns from my genetic background and releasing any stored melodrama, dogma and victim from my emotional body was my choice and became my responsibility always supported by a gracious Universe.

A whole new world opened to me as I began using bush flower essences, crystals, practising Buddhist and Transcendental Meditations, and learning how sound and colour could alter my subtle body. For years I listened to Jack Pursel who channels a spiritual teacher known as Lazaris, and learnt to become comfortable with a way of self-healing that I continue to carry through to all aspects of my life.

All these metaphysical and spiritual tools were available for me to use, to access the natural love and healing grace that I now knew resided within me, to achieve wellness and balance.

During these years I wrote in my journal daily, and would record written conversations with my guardians, guides and my higher self.

I declared to the Universe that the only information I wanted to channel was to come from the *Highest Light,* so as to protect all my bodies, especially my physical and psychic bodies. I felt it was imperative for me to learn to do this.

I had many enlightening dreams, and together with my practice of devotion to the *Highest Light,* I felt confident in asking for the guidance I knew I needed. This bought me in contact with many gifted healers, people whom I appreciate and respect. I journeyed to many powerful places to try and understand why I was here on Earth, and what it was that drove me to want to discover myself?

Then in 2010, whilst writing in my journal in my garden, I had a vision of a tall spirit being with a male appearance, dressed in a long tunic-styled robe who politely asked if I would scribe for a collection of wise ones. I was informed that this assembly was a forum of elders and would be named *Joy,* and that we would work happily together. I felt extremely honoured and agreed to be their scribe. This is how *With Love from Joy* began.

As I transcribed, if I was in any way confused about the subject being offered, I would step away. Days later I would revisit my writing and would notice that often the same message would reappear, however the subject would be written from another perspective. I became convinced I was supposed to be writing these messages.

I am deeply and sincerely grateful to a loving Universe and daily express my appreciation. I have learnt to listen, breathe and give thanks for all that I have with the assistance of *Mother Nature.*

I endeavour to stay balanced in mind body and spirit, and to translate these messages to the best of my ability. Enjoy. Moya.

Contents

How to Use This Book

THIS BOOK has been transcribed from a collection of energetic messages and captured in a timeless language. On occasion you may notice unique phrasing or discover new interpretations for words.

There are several ways to allow the words in this book to be of benefit. You may like to read through the pages from beginning to end, so as to grasp the concept of the entire collection of messages *Joy* has given us.

As you gain an understanding of the value of these passages of wisdom, you may then be inclined to use this book as a daily reference.

If you have a question, focus on it, then invite *Joy* to speak directly to you; move to a random page and there you will find your answer. The words will often seem to shape-shift, allowing a new perspective to appear between the lines, offering a unique response to your question.

The messages in this book are delivered with gentleness and compassion, inviting us to willingly and easily learn to know and appreciate *Joy.*

Wishing you a transformative experience in the company of these words.

Introduction

MOYA LOVE: I act as a conduit for a group of wise ones who wish to be named *Joy* – and when this beautiful spirit energy speaks, it does so to all who choose to listen.

We are all addressed as *Dear Heart*. I am advised there will be explanations as we go along, so I am to continue transcribing...

Joy: The fact that we name you *Dear Heart*, has deep relevance and meaning. We come to be with you and ask our scribe that she take down the details we wish written, so that we may easily convey our messages to those who will read these words. Then we have started, haven't we? So now we continue.

The message we bring is to inform all those who choose to heal that there are helpers; those of us who listen with compassion and who wish to help you with your life. Our message will always be one of hope.

We shall repeat our intention to inform you that we love you and wish to assist you in your life at all times. We are always with you.

We emphasise how loved you are. All those living an Earth existence are so deeply loved, and if you have known this before, then now we remind you of this truth.

We have chosen this one to scribe our words because she is willing and able to do so. She has the time and the temperament to assist us with our plans and this is so helpful.

We speak in the plain language of your time, with the intention of sparking interest and good sense in the lives of those who choose to live with wisdom.

We are enthusiastic and excited to be able to come this way and see our words travel across a page. So continue reading, *Dear Heart*, and we will deliver to you our warmest love and endeavour to convey a sense of trust and security so that you may become brave and adventurous.

Our Conversations

THESE CONVERSATIONS between us seem as though they are one-sided, yet this is not so. We are able to observe the habits and rituals of those in your world and it is these observations that we remark upon.

There are many who request help in the natural way of a simple heartfelt prayer, or as a son or daughter asks of a loving parent. It is to this particular group that we send answers.

Deep within the essence of all humans is a place of spirit that remembers itself as light. Many wish to become more familiar with their light-filled souls and spirits.

Their minds wander out asking questions and our *Creator* hears and so we come to fulfil our mission to inform and heal those who seek.

From the depth of personal mystery comes this cry to understand and to be understood. You are not accepting of the status quo. You are realising your personal power and remembering, even in dreams, your plans for this lifetime.

Take time to listen to yourself and your internal desires for love and wisdom. We are always here for you. Ask of us, brave ones, as we are here for you.

Joy

THIS NAME *Joy* has a mighty resonance that reaches out and includes a delightful array of energies, feelings and emotions.

Our happiness and healing love extend to include you and every aspect of your life. It is our dearest wish to be of assistance to you, *Dear Heart*, to bring you the energies of love and comfort that are desired and appreciated by those living an Earth life.

We fill our hearts with light so that you are able to feel our presence whenever you request us. We are here to assist you to feed your soul and nurture your spirit, as attention to your inner self is integral to all aspects of your life.

We are aware that you are wondering why we would include you in our light-filled existence. We have seen the struggle our Earth friends often experience and so we have chosen to become part of a great array of helpers available to assist you.

As our conversations continue, a friendly, relaxed familiarity will mature our relationship with each other, which will be of great benefit to all.

We wish that you ask of us; let us know what it is that troubles you and we will help you.

Our intention is to speak clearly and simply, that we may always surround you with confidence and *Joy*.

Lightness

WHEN YOU decide to become more of who you are, there is urgency in the initial stages for completion, and this is understandable.

With the excitement of progress and the prospect of elevation, focus and intensity become the natural elements of success.

Then the process becomes real, as gradually the body, mind and spirit align and realign with a higher vision.

We suggest that you call in the energy of patience, *Dear Heart,* requesting that you receive help to contain yourself in order to move forward step by step to reach your goal.

This passage is named lightness, so we will continue with our discourse in a light and happy manner.

To be able to communicate with you in this way brings us such pleasure, and together we continue to complement each other, as our respect and understanding strengthens.

We have a voice, and with your interest and acceptance of us into your world, we will develop with the assistance of each other. We are here to learn about your life and to offer alternatives to resistance.

You are willing to read our words so as to be united with us and learn to live life more easily.

We all come from *light* and as this realisation bonds us together, we develop feelings of trust and security between us.

We are interested in your life; we love you and respect your bravery.

Power

PUT AWAY thoughts of doubt, *Dear Heart*. Stay close to the love and light within to build an even deeper rapport with your essence.

When doubt rises, look at it as an old restriction that is now obsolete and shift your mind to the *Joy* we bring.

Grant us the pleasure of helping you with whatever it is you wish to do, as this is indeed a blessing.

Bring us your queries, placing them in our hands, with an understanding that your power remains strong. Offers of help are not in any way intended to override your will or personal decisions. We are here as a forum, in which you are able to state your case and it will be discussed freely, always respectful of your input. When the ideas have been expanded and investigated, the subject is handed back to you and the power you hold to determine an outcome.

We call this segment power, as it is our recognition of your power and the respect we have for all individuals on their journey.

Your Earth life is filled with opportunities and challenges and we commend you for your courage and bravery, as we are highly respectful of your choice to evolve in this way.

Allow us to be of assistance whenever you wish, to help create a sense of ease and lightness in your day.

Your powerful decision to ask of us will always include a willing Universe, which appreciates your decision to surmount doubt. This is a very brave and honest step and we applaud you wholeheartedly.

Wisdom

WISDOM RISES from the soul and the spirit. When it is comfortable and complete within the essence of the being, this wise power expands to include the mind.

Wisdom is deeply respectful of all aspects of the being and includes everyday occurrences and challenges that are part of a human life.

All that is required of you is to realise that wisdom lives and breathes within you, and to pause long enough for it to present itself.

We are all sparks of light, at one with our *Creator*, and within the process of evolution we come to accept this joyously. Life then takes a turn where you, *Dear Heart,* in your world, begin to develop compassion and an awareness of yourself as light.

We are not here to challenge you. We are here to present you with information, that at some time, you will be required to accept. As the conscious mind relinquishes its control over your life, the powers of higher learning simply arrive.

When this happens, all in the Universe rejoice. The *Creator* of us all wants you to heal, so choose your own way to bring about this great transformation.

We are here to say we are bringing you knowledge from the realms of wisdom. We are aware of every stage of the initiate, those who consciously decide and powerfully declare to the Universe their intention to learn more of their true self. So at your request, we willingly and lovingly guide you, allowing time for integration and acceptance, as you move through various layers of understanding.

At all times, speak to us of any dilemma that may present itself and we will offer our perspective. It is your will to elevate yourself from the old way and in this day and age, this is a courageous quest.

May we say how we love and respect you, always sending you our hope-filled blessings.

Personal Will

WE ARE here to offer our love and assistance at all times and to prompt you to continue to call on us.

It is your decision at any given time, to surrender your personal will and align with the compassionate will of our *Creator.*

This means surrendering all control of the lower mind to the higher mind that connects with the soul and spirit and so merges with the universal whole.

What could go wrong when you are connected to *God, Goddess, All That Is?*

You are safe, protected and loved always. Your desire to surrender to the conscious awareness of what it is you are doing will bring serenity and even deeper feelings of security.

Every soul, within every being wants these mystical feelings of bonding, which bring internal delight and change the way you view the world around you.

15

Often this takes practice, as opportunities for self – awareness develop within the stillness of quiet times and meditation.

Connect with the world of colour Mother Nature offers, as this provides a natural way.

Ask, Listen, Wait

WE ARE not encumbered with the restraints of an Earth life. We see the difficulty; the focus of mind and the will required to remain centred when surrounded by the unbalanced energies of others.

This is why we come to offer our guidance and light, to assist your growth toward the awareness of your true self. This is why we come.

To have chosen the life you now live, is courageous, and we applaud your endeavours.

Our mission is to come and be with you, to connect to your higher mind. This super consciousness knows ways of circumnavigating obstacles that may otherwise hinder your progress or restrict you.

Our first suggestion is to step up from the lower mind as often as your daily life permits and ask the *Highest Light* to guide you. Staying in touch with our *Creator* retains this presence in the forefront of your mind. Then when your life becomes unbalanced, for whatever reason, your automatic response will be to ask for help.

Once this is done, be *patient enough to wait and listen, knowing you have been heard*. Listen and feel our loving guidance as it surrounds you.

As you learn to surrender to your higher mind, life becomes enriched, personal maturity grows and feelings of appreciation and gratitude abound.

We Understand

WE COME from a place of learning and our life is enhanced when we visit and converse with you.

We are pleased with what we see, as those of you who decide to bloom and grow, do so with the highest intention.

There is a lot of information on your planet regarding the ways and means of healing and reaching your zenith.

We say; be aware. Truth lies within yourself and even though there are many guidelines for you to follow, they are not your essence. These guidelines have been set up by others, and represent their view of your world, so be aware of this.

Even though many of these flags of information are valuable, always come back to yourself and dig deep within. When you are willing to involve your soul this way, the passion and integrity of the spirit becomes involved, and with permission, is more able to guide.

The pretence of light and healing invades the minds of many. This often detracts from the real issues crying out to be addressed. Sometimes, due to shame, it is not easy to reveal personal issues.

This shame is born and even bred by ideas passed down from other generations that impede life as it is now. Sort out what is relevant and leave the past behind.

There is so much love, light, help and healing grace available; why would you always wish to refer to the past? Acknowledge your experiences as history and move on.

The cleansing that is taking place in your world today is providing excellent opportunities for renewal and our message is to say how sincerely we wish to assist.

We see your world, we understand, and we are here to bring you our light and wisdom. We are all sparks of light that bounded off from the original source of light. As *Joy,* we are detached from your subjective world and come from this pure source of light and love, offering to help you remember who you truly are.

The Beauty of a Woman

WE ARE aware that some people create drama in their lives. There are many ways to learn to override the fear that causes your thinking to change from being a dramatic assessment of a situation, to a clear practical process.

If you would become aware, *Dear Heart,* that the view you have of your life is often one of fear and concern, this awareness then highlights the process you may wish to change.

Many women, may we say, are burdened by emotional anxiety and this clouds the pure light of their wise, decision-making ability.

The nature of a woman is especially creative. In the past, this creativity has not been respected to the degree that allows the feminine aspect of a woman to be pure. Now we have arrived at a time when this is being corrected, and so the power of the feminine in the woman is returned to her and she is again, complete.

We see women gauging their beauty on outside influences and tastes. This can create a very limited version of your truth, as we will explain.

We see beauty as the movement of a woman as she goes through her day. Her deep nurturing ways; reaching out to succour others, are steeped in beauty, even if she is unaware of this.

We see beauty in the intention of a woman to be whole and feminine, living her life, delving into her own mystery. She most always includes others with her genuine desire to care and comfort. How could this not be beautiful?

Women are so beautiful. You are so beautiful, *Dear Heart*. We would love all women to turn inward, and discover their personal mystery and all the secrets that lie therein.

It has been a long time since women have been revered and respected, and now the tide is turning. With an appreciation of the purity and joy that lies within, the essence of beauty becomes the woman.

Good Humour

WELCOME *Dear Heart*, and what a beautiful day it is!

We look at this day with eyes that see all the beauty and goodness that surrounds us. We smile to ourselves and ask you to smile also. This is not difficult you know, and creates such a place of pleasure and relief in your mind.

Smile, that's the way, it is easier whatever the circumstances and the effect of smiling and light-heartedness brings us closer.

We also say, having a big belly laugh sends waves of humour generously to all around you, as this vibrant, enthusiastic energy spreads good cheer.

You know, it's not difficult to focus on the effect good humour produces and sometimes when you may not be attuned to this mood, if you will at least look and listen, magic happens.

Speaking of magic, it's in the smile of a woman, in the touch of a child and in the tenderness of all those who care. Magic, laughing, humour, and smiling together celebrate the wholesomeness of life as it was designed.

We are so honoured to be visiting and loving you today. We appreciate that you are reading these words and smiling – yes, we can see you. We delight, as this smile lifts your spirit and so invites health and happiness in abundance.

You are beautiful, *Dear Heart*. Your intentions are divine, and the love we have for you has no bounds.

Ask of us, we are with you.

Enjoy your day.

Competition

THE MANY differences of opinion on subjects raised every day allow you to ascertain your own level of understanding for any given situation. You are sometimes faced with a dilemma when you reach out to offer your opinion. Be aware that you are also reaching out into the minds of others.

Doing the best you can is all you are required to do at any given time.

Your perception of the value of life, and how this understanding reveals itself, continues to display new and varied aspects. This is all part of the process of learning.

There is no right way for anything. You are all in stages of personal growth and self-recognition. It is your innate knowing that clarifies a situation.

Be brave with yourself, as you accept that what you may believe to be true at this moment may be superseded and dissolved by bubbles of light-filled illumination.

Relax into your life and as peace and calm reign, your willingness to allow others their views will be an opportunity and a gift.

We see you all struggling to keep up with each other and we smile as this is impossible. All the soul wants is attention to the inner self.

Competition and an upbeat attitude does not always equate to being right. You are not required to follow any rules. Remaining focused and balanced is enough. With this sense of equilibrium gently installed, the magic of personal intuition easily provides knowing and guidance. From this layer of understanding, if it is your intention, then your higher mind gradually presents life from a universal perspective.

Be aware of the changes in energy that permeate your day, gently acquiescing to this knowledge.

It is unnecessary to compete, merely be with your own presence and its patient progress.

Inspiration

WE WISH to speak about inspiration and the high levels of light energy that transpire between those who generate and those who receive this vitality.

Now, *Dear Heart*, we offer this idea of inspiration to you to expand this concept and include more of this powerful force.

If you would look around and absorb inspiration from Mother Earth, duly acknowledge the bounty that is produced for the betterment of mankind, you will be inspired to achieve. To watch the Earth producing is, in itself, inspirational.

To see people around you who inspire from the highest levels of their being, lifts your heart and spirit and urges you on to your next step. To read books written by inspirational people with messages of hope and encouragement, will often deliver just the right words that you have been looking for.

We all know this is one of the ways the Universe succeeds in transmitting uplifting energy around the natural world. Those who have awareness accept and acknowledge this, allowing these inspirational moments to change their lives.

This is our *Creator* creating and we, as members of this universal family, gratefully accept and receive this loving kindness.

We offer these suggestions to you today, *Dear Heart,* as we know you will absorb them to the best of your ability. Your individuality is respected and valued.

Thank you again for your time with us.

Love always.

Respect

WE ARE here to offer suggestions and new perspectives. We are not here to rule your will or infringe upon your guidance system in any way. Our respect for the path you have chosen, and the way in which you live within the world around you, fills us with admiration.

We come as friends, willing to discuss ideas that flow out around the Universe and have caught your attention. When these energetic thought forms find their way into your orbit and stimulate your interest, then this is when we also wish to join in with these conversations.

Our willingness and wisdom combine to produce wonderful philosophical discussions, which we enjoy immensely. We know that this is not the end, nor is it the solution to this discussion. We are all aware that as we evolve, so does information, truth and wisdom. As this subject is presented, let us ponder the understanding that together we are discovering more about each other and the Universe in which we live. The ability to be able to move into the intelligence of the higher mind offers peaceful, secure solutions to life.

Together we become informed and exchange ideas back and forth from each other, revealing the soul's intention to evolve.

The spirit and soul within, *Dear Heart* are able to communicate with us this way, relaxed and feeling safe within the light energy that is produced between us.

These days, you are more aware of the difference between where you have been and your desires for the future. This plays a great part in your way forward, as you often taste the freedom the higher mind reveals.

Our collective ideas and suggestions unite us and deepen our friendship, with the sole purpose of continuing to listen and to respect each other.

These courtesies between us generate wholeness and balance. We have included ourselves in this discourse as we wish you to know, *Dear Heart*, how much we learn from you in your life with its daily decisions. We are always here for you, with the greatest respect.

Perceptions

WHEN YOU request of us *Dear Heart*, we listen. As your beliefs change from doubt and apprehension to acceptance and trust, we are more able to make contact with you in a way that assists and pacifies you.

This exchange of asking and receiving is real. When the call goes out, hold the thought. The time it takes for the return of energy requires stillness, together with patience and faith that your petition has been heard and is being answered.

There is no mystery as to why some people seem to receive more than others. It requires a deep and humble desire by individuals, and their respect for us, to manifest light and clarity.

All people are different in their ability to receive our love. Often answers come unexpectedly, as our perception of your request may differ from yours. The more you understand our individual connection, the easier it is for us to align with you and your life.

You are surrounded by love at all times. We will continue to say these words again and again, until one day with our grace and hope for you, this truth will be accepted.

We are here for you and for everyone. We have an understanding that your mind contains a lot of irrelevant chatter. We are also aware that part of your evolutionary process is to cleanse and master your thoughts and so we offer our hand to you.

This is what we live for; this is our mission, to bring you words of truth and to remind you to remember who you are.

Love and Comfort

WE COME to commune with you in a relaxed, easy manner, so as to have wonderful conversations and develop the love and trust that assists us both.

We wish to companion you, *Dear Heart*, to be a source of comfort and security, always available whenever you are perplexed.

We take advantage of this opportunity to present our wisdom in this manner, so we are more easily able to communicate with you. If at any time you wish to ask of us, we are willing to be of assistance.

Today's message is a reminder; even when you are on your own, we are always with you, as the natural world is ever present. Sometimes this is forgotten as you go about your daily tasks.

When life presents difficulties, ask of us to prepare a way forward for you, as we are then able to give you our support and encouragement.

We urge you to become aware of our presence. We are part of the unseen world, yes? We are also part of Mother Nature and the natural world. So if you would expand your imagination to include the greater Universe then you will find yourself deeply embraced in our love and comfort.

We see you looking down at the pavement when you walk. Look up and smile, as this movement lifts the spirit and sends light filled messages to the brain. The Universe loves the symbols you register and duly responds.

Have a wonderful day.

Your Garden

THE DELIGHT you receive from your garden, with its produce, brings natural feelings of achievement.

The combination of the generosity of the Earth and your intention to plant and gather intensifies your affinity for the land. You are aware, *Dear Heart*, that plants and animals live within their kingdoms to enhance the planet.

Respect and honour them for their existence permits a familiarity with sacredness, as you allow yourself to be part of their world.

The Earth, even with its robust nature, requires sustenance and tender care. With the mind and hands of a gardener, you can readily provide this consideration.

You are now aware that the attentiveness paid to your particular garden is rewarded with feelings of jubilation, when each day you notice the effect of your eagerness to cultivate.

Working in your garden, tending carefully and thoughtfully to your soil, deepens your loving awareness.

Your willingness to include Mother Earth in your daily routine brings contentment, as the soil reciprocates and provides.

When a day's gardening is complete, having worked together with vegetables, plants and trees to bring health and vitality to their needs, one's inner self also feels replenished.

This is such a simple undertaking, and to those who work on the land, the complexities of existence are muted, as their desire to love, care for and provide, retains their focus with Mother Nature.

The Earth is generous and will always give, as its mission is to yield and replenish.

Your Essence

THE SOUL and spirit that inhabit the body require little encouragement when asked to guard and to guide. You have arrived at this moment of understanding. Congratulations!

May we say how delighted we are, to be with you today, *Dear Heart*, as our pleasure deepens with every conversation we have together.

As you move through the necessary layers of understanding to reach yet another level, we suggest that as well as becoming aware of what it is you are doing, it will be wise to hand over your transformation to the Universe.

Does the Universe know who I am and the status of my evolution? Yes it does and with the continued practice of asking, then knowing you are heard, you will more easily trust when you hear or feel responses.

You made the decision to incorporate another lifetime into your story, as a way of completing and healing that which was entangled.

37

When you decide that you have done enough, you will surrender this idea of lifetime after lifetime and accept you are love in its purest form. Turn now, more often to the soul and let your essence be your guide.

Reassurance

LET US just relax and be easy in our journey together.

Let us become more familiar with each other, deepening and strengthening our closeness. *Dear Heart*, together we lift your spirit with our *Joy*. This is why we come to be with you.

We could even call ourselves an insulation from the outside world and what is happening around you. Come in and read these words and feel our deep intention to be true to you; as we say, we love you.

Let this be a simple message of reassurance that the love that we are is close to you wherever you live and whatever you do. Let yourself ponder a moment or two on these words. Even though you do not see us, we send you feelings of deep commitment from the words that we write, to assure you of our constant presence.

We love you deeply *Dear Heart*, spending our days watching over you and surrounding you with light. As you ask more of us, then it is entirely possible for us to come even closer, so that we may whisper to you quietly and gently.

As you become familiar with us and your trust grows, you will develop more awareness of how we are able to intercede in your life, for whatever reason you ask.

We are able to be with you in an instant. It takes your willingness to allow us to be together and your realisation that we are able to assist you, even in the simplest of tasks.

Your decision is at the request of your willing spirit and we have the utmost respect for this, your gift.

We will continue to come to be with you this way, to reassure you of our love and devotion to you. As the old ways crumble and fall, then our friendship and trust will grow and so we become united, eternally.

Bless you.

Gratitude

OUR GRATITUDE is beyond words.

We will continue to express ourselves with gratefulness and genuine pleasure, as this is our nature.

Dear Heart, our presence in your life is with your permission and we have come to value our time with you.

To continue opening to deeper feelings of gratitude at this time is entirely relevant, as we see huge spaces of energy in the world around you that if filled with gratitude would change many lives.

We would love to convey to you how euphoric and elevated you will feel when you learn to see your world with eyes full of love and gratitude.

Everything human, animal, plant and mineral, are treasured and valued by the Universe.

Taking care of yourself in the simplest way, with the intention of bringing balance and nurturing, is the recognition your body requires. Moments of devotion, acts of kindness, time spent doing physical exercise, all add up to the understanding; this is who I Am.

As you reach yet another level on your journey, look back for a moment with forgiveness, compassion and gratitude. The past is the past and the way forward beckons.

To conclude our conversation, we suggest that you pause each day, recognise what it is you have achieved and feel the thrill of knowing you are a combination of all aspects of your being. The acknowledgement of this process deepens the gratitude that emanates from your soul, and realigns you with our *Creator*.

Encouragement

WRITING AND reading our words inspires all of us, as we develop a sense of union, gratefully feeling the appreciation of love.

We come to be with you so as to accompany you on your way and to offer another perspective. We say again how powerful you are, and how we do not come to tell you how to live your life.

We write these words as we have been given this opportunity and understand the courageous life you inhabit.

Your light beams guide us to you at every moment and this relationship connects us as family.

We welcome you and greet you with love. Members, those light-filled ones that inhabit an Earth body, and who are aware of the miracles and magic that surround them, register their intention with us that they wish to stay informed. This calls us, and we provide our services to the individual needs of those who wish us to confer with them.

You are all filled with light and wisdom and have chosen to be Earth-bound to release yourself from veils that may cloud your vision.

Dear Heart, your decision to experience this Earth life, is because there are issues to be healed. As the process continues, remember your support comes from strength, light and grace.

We commend you, *Dear Heart*, for your devotion to the completion of wholeness and the integration of your mind, body, soul and spirit.

Feel the pleasure that fulfilment brings, as you endeavour to reach yet another stage of human and spiritual maturity.

Still Inner Self

DEAR HEART, remaining grounded and balanced keeps your energies stabilised and focused.

We understand that taking little periods of rest between our conversations, to allow the senses to absorb and adjust, invites new information to be fully integrated.

We will continue happily chatting as often as you come to read, as we love to be with you this way.

The idea that your world is separate from other worlds is a myth and promotes disbelief and confusion, as our world of light, love and wisdom continues to blend with you and yours.

Though there is often much chaos and many disturbances around you, the *still self* recognises our presence and wishes contact.

Paying attention to this *divine inner being* brings together the yearnings of the soul, the desires of the heart and the practical intelligence of the mind. This is happiness and joy expressing itself.

When issues are raised around you, your growing sense of personal intimacy, that holds the key to your relationship with your *still inner self,* will create a balance between the chaos and calm.

This recognition of your soul and spirit develops confidence, and presents a way of life where your reliance on your inner knowing guides your way. This takes faith and a dedication to the fulfilment of personal destiny.

The wise power of self-love and respect becomes a constant reference point in your everyday life.

Bubbles of Light

WHEN WE are with each other, we continue to express our gratitude with sincerity.

As our lives intermingle, and your thoughts and ours become supportive of each other, we are more able to view your desires.

The position you hold in the world and the place where you live, often determines the responses we will make in answer to your queries.

Your particular circumstances may be viewed by yourself and others as beyond your comprehension, yet we are able to see your situation more clearly.

When you include us in your daily aspirations, we enthusiastically attend to your ideas, and in moments of quiet and calm, you are then able to register our signals.

As *light energy* and the growth of trust clear the path between us, we enjoy a relationship with your spirit that has been destined.

We come and speak plainly, so as to develop and deepen your security, which we hope will assist in overriding the culture of fear that surrounds you.

We suggest you allow yourself to look at this fear and regard it as outside of your wish for love and happiness.

Meditate daily with *bubbles of white light* and the fear will subside, as it is ever present in your world. Many others regularly exercise this practice, so look to their examples to follow.

Thank you for your time with us today, *Dear Heart*. We continue to be with you, gently guiding at your request as you explore your creativity.

Recreate

RELAX, *Dear Heart*, life supports you and the guidance and love of the Universe is here to stay. Many changes will take place as you go about your daily life, with the intention of including your soul and spirit in your activities. When you are unaware of this revelation, you are more prone to disbelief and confusion. Your soul is your greatest friend, and calls *Itself, I Am.*

This presence resides within your body and is connected to our *Creator,* who watches over you every moment of every day. This is the real world and the truth of this is the awakening that has been happening for many years. It has been gradual and has passed through many stages and barriers, yet as you read these words it is again changing and presenting itself even more clearly.

The evolution of your personal Universe, *Dear Heart,* co-creates with the evolution of the entire Universe, so we say trust in your instincts and knowing, allowing *Great Spirit* to guide. With this in mind the thinking brain understands it is unable to supply all the answers and is willing to rest. When it does, the soul brain, with its divine intelligence, supplies greater light, energy and illumination.

The practical brain will then accept that this combination produces a magical life.

Greater self-security exists within, as you learn to depend on and to trust your inner voice. Security in the world around you develops as you feel your internal guidance magnetising to you everything you need. To be able to do this is a matter of releasing old practices and learning to move out of the way.

This reassessment of yourself and your willingness to change may create confusion within, as old routines try to persist. It is very practical to have a symbol nearby to refer to. Light a candle, hold a crystal, or use coloured incense to clear the air around you or walk and exercise. All these actions make your personal intentions clear to the Universe.

Write out your goals, resolving to recreate the way you desire your life to unfold. Then give this message over to the *Creator* of our Universe with faith.

New Imagination

DEAR HEART, allow us to assist you, to look at how it is possible to use your imagination to re-create a new life. You have many pictures and stories of how it has been; now let us show you how to conjure up, as if by magic, a new way of imagining your life and your world.

If you continue to look at the routine of your life and expect this to be maintained, then *Dear Heart*, it will do so. Grant yourself the freedom to change and we will assist you to imagine a new way.

Firstly we will encourage you to clear and widen the screen of your imagination. Move the outer edges of your vision till your entire internal vista is filled with this space.

Now paint a gentle background colour onto this new image.

Smooth out this tincture to the very edges of your vision. This allows the strength and beauty of your new insight to create a filter of discernment, through which the old way is unable to penetrate.

Now imagine a scene that is tranquil and calm then gratefully add love and respect to this beautiful place.

Your soul and spirit will now show you how they wish to be part of your new life.

Continue looking at the centre of your internal screen, and ask your true self to show you your next step. What will this be? Let it be a genuine desire for happiness, love and joy.

There are many bubbles of jest and laughter swirling around onto your screen, mingling with all your background images as this idea resonates.

Balance appears, as both sides of your internal imagination automatically respond. There is a security of purpose, a deep understanding of being loved by the Universe, a willingness to co-create and a genuine desire for fulfilment.

We take time now for this to integrate as you become one with your new imagination.

Then we suggest you build an image of how you see your particular talents as a visual guide.

Include the company of like-minded friends, and an enthusiastic desire to produce work that will excite and illuminate.

To enhance this image, widen your vision to embrace a wholesome life, genuinely enjoying every day and being grateful for this opportunity to heal with hope and grace.

Place your secret wish here

....

....

....

....

....

....

If you notice, the edges of your screen curl a little, we suggest that the mastery of mental discipline is required, so as to produce all of the above.

Oh, so beautiful! Enjoy your new life.

Learning to Stabilise

DEAR HEART, you have decided to incorporate respect and beauty into your love spectrum, and this favours you well. As the full meaning and depth of these principles manifest themselves, we see life changing around you.

A sense of the whole, balanced, secure self comes from the centre of your being and this truth expands. As these changes integrate into the sense of self from the old way, you may start to panic and become anxious. You do not know what is on the other side of your conditioned learning, though remember, we all experience these feelings as we evolve.

There is a light around us that guides us, and it does so from this inner core of our being and it stays with us always.

When you are feeling the tremble of uncertainty, acknowledge its presence and choose strength, courage and light.

All is Well

54

DEAR HEART, welcome to another day.

We are interested, as we notice ever-changing events in your world. Situations around you are more ambivalent than usual, as Mother Earth exercises her disquiet, in line with planetary energies.

Your soul and spirit comprehend this process. Yet as you are human, these upheavals cause a degree of fear and drama. It is natural for you to endeavour to process what is happening around you, and it is our mission to come to you constantly and to remind you of our presence and willing companionship.

Then, times of peace and calm will come into your life, with big sunny, balmy days, quiet winds and feelings of; *'all is well in my world'*. You experience these beautiful, loving days, to balance out those times that challenge and demand your strength and practical expertise.

Be kind and considerate to yourself, respecting that even though some days are busy and tumultuous, others bring respite, and answer your prayers for peace.

Being aware and accepting life with its undulations, affords a mature, wise, standpoint from which to step out each day.

Our *Creator* wants you to heal and enjoy. Our *Creator* wants you to laugh and have fun, so focus on this often during your day, remembering this is how the Divine Will wishes you to live.

Simplicity

THE SIMPLICITY of our messages comes with our deepest admiration.

You are aware of life around you with its demands, yet at times you tend to forget the simple life-style.

We refer to the willingness of the Universe to support you. Your choice is to ask for guidance and help. The simple act of sitting up against a tree and revelling in the power of its support has the ability to calm and stabilise you.

All elements of nature are available to sustain and nurture you. Stay with clear, uncomplicated thoughts on how to go about your day, always sending the light before you. This ensures a trouble free passage.

Keep the mind powerful with the desire for light, love and happiness, whatever your mission. As these thought patterns develop, your life will magically transform itself.

Dear Heart, endeavour to sustain inner peace with the idea of being one with the Universe, including us in your desires.

Set up your own support system, tuning in at all times and developing from your soul and spirit a simple faith that life will always encourage you. This way of thinking and organising your day-to-day activities retains the focus on staying centred and balanced.

Whatever level of life you lead, in whatever profession or place you have chosen to live, remember you are soul and spirit, as well as body and mind.

This mature recognition respects life around you and welcomes opportunities to remain abundant and fruitful at all times.

Such a simple way, yet there have been years of learning that life is a struggle, so now we offer you this suggestion: Take back your own power of self – love and respect and choose your preferred way, and simply, live.

Personal Resolve

WE ARE here with you again *Dear Heart,* loving the way you live your life.

You are not in your world to be perfect. We say this with a great desire to impress upon you this truth. Your perfection is understood to always be present, as you have been designed and moulded by our *Creator.*

When you are listening to all the insecurity, instability and gossip around you, it is difficult to retain a true image of yourself.

This then raises doubt in your abilities and you are distracted by the intentions and emotions of others, creating chasms of confusion that pull you off course from your original path.

It is with our deepest love that we entreat you to look at this part of your humanity.

Know yourself, your gifts and desires for your life.

Stay with these insights, developing your adventurous and enthusiastic self that wishes to explore the world around you.

When you find yourself being pulled away from your true essence, halt the process, become still and choose.

Return to your own path, understanding that your perfection is between your *true self* and our *Creator* and this bond is without question.

Should others speak to you or imply that you are not the way you know you are, then take a mental step back and choose to stay true to yourself.

Allow others to have their opinions, remembering they are on their path, not yours. With maturity, it is essential that you realise this.

Value your ideas, what you achieve, where you have been, and how strong you are in your personal resolve. Become courageous as you build your own world, with all the personal integrity that you possess.

A Changing World

DEAR HEART, you live in such a wonderful world.

At this time, so many people are developing awareness and exercising their rights as humans to live the way they wish to live.

This may not always be seen within the bounds of conventional wisdom, though it is the way in which these young people are exercising their power.

Some who release themselves from old ways may be inclined to become unbalanced in their effort to move far from the prisoner-like-mentality that has been thrust up on them in the past.

People often act the way they are treated and so conflict emerges, as they are seen as radicals in their attempt to rid themselves of restriction as old bonds are severed.

Many people during their lifetimes completely comprehend that they are not the people they have been told they are, or the image that society has thrust upon them.

Whether this understanding is significant enough for them to change, seek help, and move to higher ground, is their choice.

Sometimes only small windows of light appear and people realise; this is the way I wish to go and I prefer to follow my way. Others also see these windows of light, though they fear stepping outside their practised traditions.

The more people realise they are not alone, and that our love and guidance is available to them, the braver they become as they acknowledge the presence of *Joy*.

People want happiness, fulfilment, abundance and a rich and rewarding life. How individuals endeavour to achieve these heartfelt desires is a personal choice and often influenced by their surroundings.

Those who look up and out, seeking opportunities with bravery, open their hearts and spirits to a way of evolution now prevalent in your world. These are wholesome times; take advantage of every opportunity and gift yourself daily.

Achievement

ACHIEVEMENT, with the accomplishment of the simplest of tasks, arouses feelings of raised hope and a renewed sense of contentment.

We wish to speak about achievement in such a way as to deliver ideas of raising the vision of your possible futures to another level.

The time has come for all those who feel a lightness of heart to expect more from themselves and to look around for yet further ways of exercising their creative intelligence.

Dear Heart, some people achieve continuously and live lives of expression and fulfilment. There are many more lovely people who are so easily able to delve within, conquer personal fears and look closely at the world around them. In doing so, they expand their imagination in order to implement further opportunities. Then there are those who will negate this suggestion, as they do not feel encouragement from a support body ready to stimulate and reassure them.

This is why we are here to be your universal champions, always ready and willing to companion and intercede for you, in whatever it is you are willing to achieve.

The only thing that is required is to ask us to accompany you. Follow your instinctual urges towards your goal, listen as we will be with you, and together we create. With your permission we are able to join with you in manifesting an original idea and with flexibility bring this to fruition.

Choose what you wish to achieve. Then with introspection and honesty, realise what it is that stands in your way.

Then look into your practical mind; has it given you permission? When this is granted move down into your heart-mind and soul-brain and decide to follow your inner guidance, allowing clarity to form within the expression of your new ideas.

The Universe will always support you. Include us in your plans.

Moving Forward

DEAR HEART, everyone is unique, complete with their individual skills and gifts, all waiting to be revealed and appreciated.

If you would imagine how valuable you are and see yourself as we do, you would give up your drudgery in an instant.

You are all filled with light and have chosen an Earth lifetime to evolve spiritually. Yet you focus on the importance of material gain, as you believe this will bring you the security you so ardently desire.

We elected to come and have our words transcribed because we wish to remind you that the primary reason you chose your Earth life at this time was to move further away from the fear and closer to the love.

If you will pause for a few moments each day, centre yourself between your head and your soul, and confidently move to this position of intuitive understanding, faith and trust will grow. This is such a pleasurable experience.

All it takes is a recreation of internal practices and a personal desire to generate compassion and love for self. With respect, understand you chose to be here in the first place.

We come because you called us. We come because there are so many seeking answers in a world that seems to be in constant confusion and insecurity.

Recognise fear when it raises its head and do not allow it to sway you from your purest self.

We say with all sincerity that out of chaos comes calm and a new way, so make use of our presence, call on us, and together we will move forward into the future.

A Rich Rewarding Life

YOUR THOUGHTS go before you with the intention of designing a rich and rewarding life. This description requires action, faith, trust in self, and a clear desire to include the support of the Universe.

Yes?

We see that to be able to achieve, balance is paramount at every turn.

Dear Heart, self-mastery with the energies of physical agility, mental peace, emotional and spiritual poise, is required to integrate and deliver ideas and information to all parts of your being.

If a rich and rewarding life be your intention, continue, knowing that you will always be presented with possibilities, probabilities and opportunities.

When your ideas are filled with passion and desire, enjoy your progress and realise how fortunate you are to be able to rise above that which you have been taught.

Live in the times of the day, accepting of all powerful openings presented to you. Such a wonderful lifestyle and it is available to everyone.

This is an exciting project that you have taken on with us, *Dear Heart,* and we are so thrilled to come and converse with you in a plain and simple language that will lift your heart.

Our dearest wish is that you will listen to our words, with the faith and sincere love in which we deliver them. Allow us into your world with permission to accompany you.

This is all we ask. You are all so courageous and brave. Remember, at any time of the day or night we are here for you.

Money

WHAT A pleasure it is, *Dear Heart*, to share ideas with you. We see you in your world doing the best you can and we applaud all that you do.

We are generous in our praise for you, as we know your world requires you to be responsible for every aspect of your living. Today we take notice of the financial situation of your planet and how the cost of living has accelerated, with the exchange of goods and services rapidly rising.

We are sympathetic to the unstable monetary position of the times. Many, who are not at all schooled in the skill of forecasting their financial futures, gratify themselves continuously and this may be to their detriment.

Money is a spiritual asset and when viewed in this way, will always be available to assist you, to live life easily and to provide for all your needs. Move away from the fear of money with its connotations of lack, and life changes around you.

Respect money as it is a powerful force that refuses to be contained.

Honour the lifestyle that the flow of money brings, gratefully calling on the abundance of the Universe to continue supplying all areas of life for self and others. This acknowledgment of the spiritual aspect of money alters the context of a currency exchange.

There are various ideas of thought regarding money. Some may believe it brings happiness, some want money to use as revenge, and others, to acquire power. Many are relaxed and trusting, as they have reconciled themselves to the circulation of money they have been fortunate enough to manifest, and confidently expect this to continue.

Our intention of raising this subject today is to create the awareness that money is a great and powerful spiritual asset. The understanding is that the balance between acknowledging this spiritual resource, with the relevant practical necessities of living life, creates a source of continuous supply.

Love

HOW DO we find words that will describe love?

It is the air you breathe, the breath you take, the gratitude you acknowledge for the life you live.

Love is remembering you are light and that every cell in your being consists of light and love, as you are fashioned by our *Creator*.

Unconditional love is the acceptance by your mind that, as soul and spirit, you are sons and daughters of a light-filled love, so perfect and whole.

Love is walking the Earth with feelings of security and pleasure, smiling to yourself, knowing you came to enjoy this experience.

Love is intimacy with self, respect and acceptance of self, always forgiving and cleansing then returning to feelings of worthiness and value.

Love is living your life in whatever profession or field of endeavour you have chosen, and delighting in everything and everyone that surrounds you.

Love is enjoying a pleasurable relationship with self, your soul, spirit and *Creator*, often relishing quiet times together.

Love is the acceptance of others and the way they choose to live their lives. It is respecting self enough to let others be as they are and choosing to stay within your own divine essence.

The life we live is all about love. You came to find love firstly within yourself. Appreciating and honouring self, then others, creates an ambiance of love that initiates compassion and grace.

Loving self connects us with the *Quintessence Itself* to the intimacy of the *quintessence* within.

Love is the source of all freedom and so much more. It is a willingness to allow the powers of life to open your heart, mind and soul to the truth of your personal destiny.

Love and Joy continue to guide and guard you every step of the way.

A Summary

DEAR HEART, we come with our wisdom and our learning because you called. We come to surround you with the warmth of our presence, to accompany you, and to impress upon you that the love we have for you is unparalleled.

Your Earth life includes us, your friendly companions, and we are deeply respectful of your decision to be present, living, and manifesting your life. Some of you feel as though your life is in order, and this is wonderful, we congratulate you.

Some feel daily imbalance, allowing fear to flow through your minds, disturbing and distracting your forward progress. Whatever your personal level of understanding, sustain your bravery and courage, by remembering the *love and joy* of the spirit within.

This is why you came to Earth. This is why we are here, to ask you to remember your connection to our *Creator*, and the unconditional love that is always present and available to you.

Your intention for this lifetime was made when you were surrounded by the light of grace and hope. We come to remind you that at the time you made your decision, you knew your destiny.

We are now able to assist you to remember your unique path, and we are delighted to be able to do this.

Spend time with us during your day. Sit quietly, moving deeply inside, and ask of us to be with you, and we will respond. The more you do this, the easier it will be for you to realise our presence, and the more intimate our conversations will become.

We feel this summary is necessary, as we see your life moving quickly and the processes that are required of you are challenging and demanding.

We come with love and compassion, to remind you of our presence and at any time of the day or night, you are most welcome to bring us into your life.

The Joy of Giving

WE ARE unseen, though this does not mean that we are invisible. Our messages beam to you through every available medium of communication.

Many of you realise this and see the answer to your query on the sides of buses and chuckle to yourself as you express your heartfelt gratitude. We are also able to speak through the voices of the friends you trust. As our relationship grows, we will bring answers in your dreams, through the call of a bird, the sounds of animals, or the whisper of soft breezes. This way you are able to see, feel and hear the effect of our association with you.

We enjoy being together and delight in the acknowledgement and appreciation you show us for our dedication. We sincerely wish to bring light-heartedness to your world and to raise the levels of joy and laughter within your day. Some people know this and respond in their own secret way, allowing us to work and play with them so readily. Others require this written explanation and we are so fortunate to be able to use these words.

The further we reach out and nurture others, the lighter and brighter our glow extends.

There are people that surround you who would jest at these ideas of communication with the Spirit World, so here we suggest you keep it your secret. If at any time people want to know what, how or who guides and guards you, then it is your choice as to how much you wish to reveal of yourself.

If you give out information prematurely, before you have accepted our sincere and honest connection, you may show your uncertainty and so be labelled as mistaken and the knowing that you hold may be misrepresented.

Your energy levels will drop when this occurs and you will find yourself weak and hampered by the disbelief others hold. Keep your own secrets so as to retain personal power and respect. We surround everyone. We are part of the love and light you breathe, and we are known to many enthusiastic people who choose joyfully to include us in their lives.

Wholesomeness

DEAR HEART, living your life with the intention of developing a wholesome sense of self, initiates the process towards calm and serenity.

Listening to our stories, with the inclusion of your input, develops wise and mature reasoning.

As the heart grows and fills with a natural realisation of the possibility of contentment and wholesomeness, thoughts of fear and insecurity vanish.

There is so much to say about the idea of wholesomeness, as this state of mind extends to all areas of life.

The food you eat, your friends, acquaintances, and Mother Nature with her powerful presence, all heighten your awareness and desire to grow with grace and hope.

Your sense of decency towards self and others creates a purity of mind that allows genuine feelings of love and respect.

As maturity deepens with the allowing of self-appreciation, all aspects of your being cooperate with your natural talents, allowing innate discernment to pave the way.

Trusting in yourself this way, creates a sense of wholesomeness you learn to depend on. The practical situations that are all part of your life become easier, as the active mind has time to rest and quieten.

The Universe watches, assisting you, as you create a life that presents itself as willing to be part of the whole.

Willingness

YOU ARE willing, yet you feel you are weak!

To be willing is to be strong and having made this brave choice, you are more likely to continue to explore and expand your willingness.

The opportunities that present themselves float through the air around you, every moment of your day. As your mind settles and accepts willingness, the clouds of fear that have been as a fog lift and dissolve, highlighting ideas and possible opportunities.

Sometimes these ideas are glimmers of hope and are enough to excite and propel you to investigate. As you delve further, you may decide that an idea is not for you and let it go. This is exercising the skill of discrimination, ever mindful of how you wish to steer the course of your life.

Original ideas and creative suggestions circulate in your atmosphere constantly.

With discrimination and positive selection you are able, intuitively, to choose a particular creative pursuit that suits your life and so add to the dreams for your future.

Understanding this perspective of how creative thought manifests, allows personal insight into your willingness.

Loving, accepting and enjoying yourself, develops the peace of knowing that any idea may be investigated, developed, carried, or dropped and released for another to pursue.

So willingness as seen from this perspective, shows itself as strong and powerful, with due respect for all the possibilities it holds.

Sending Light

AS THE heart fills and sends out light, we see how, in asking for healing grace for others, you become filled with more light and love yourself. The acknowledgment of what it is you are achieving, secures your true self and links you more consciously to our *Creator.*

Dear Heart, this simple act of sending bubbles of brightness to your friends and family, and to those who are living in the chaos of fire and flood, continues the stream of strength and hope to so many. The simplicity of this compassionate act is delivered with deep sincerity.

The light and love you transmit never goes astray and always reaches those who have called for help. This process creates a wide circle of giving and receiving and in return replenishes and secures your own light-filled thought-forms. The radiance of light energy is powerfully healing, full of magic and mysterious love, and to send this to others near and far directs a flow of widespread brilliance.

Know that when you focus this curative power, it surrounds and fills all those you have nominated, as well as offering great benefit to others.

By instigating this process, the *Brothers and Sisters of Light* lift your intentions and distribute them. This is a universally co-operative process.

Think big when sending these illuminating intentions, as the greater your vision, the more light will be radiated and the further and deeper will be its effectiveness.

Trust in yourself and the wonder of this blending, knowing that when your objective is pure, so are the rays of white light that are created.

Often you will see the effect of your giving. Smile with gratitude, keep your secret, and fall deeper in love with our *Creator*.

Welcome

WE ARE aware that the combinations of the human body, mind and psyche, often become unbalanced and will deliver an unexpected solution in the form of physical ill health. This, if it continues for a short time, will be effectively seen as an opportunity to reassess your life. Should this imbalance continue, other methods are in place so as to centre the mind, body and soul.

We are a universal forum with members who are available to be consulted. Should this be required, then it is permitted that you refer to us as *Joy*.

We are here with respect, sending out our messages in this way, to those who may wish to make contact with us and to discuss their lives.

We are always happy to listen, and depending on your ability to receive, to answer you in the most suitable way.

Listen for us, as we will always respond to your request, be assured of this.

So again, may we express our love and encouragement to you on this day.

We always watch over those who request our presence, and though we do not live your lives for you, as part of our spiritual consent, we are here waiting to assist you at any time.

Thank you again for your loving contact.

Awakening

WE SEE that you are deeply in love with the Earth around you and we see the Earth reciprocating with pleasure in your presence. This relationship with Mother Nature and her ways assists and magnifies the development of trust, truth and faith, for there lies pure power in all Her majesty.

This is a complete relationship, *Dear Heart*. Yet we see you pondering, as often our Mother Earth delivers chaos, and it is this you are trying to fathom. Please don't!

Be aware that the presence of nature, of light and love, are mysteries and should you find yourself involved within the extremities of these energies, we entreat you to come to your centre, hold still and ask for guidance.

We often see you thinking, 'it is not up to me to know the mind of *God/Goddess*'. When you completely accept this, your ways and attitudes will surrender to the security of the love and truth that surrounds you, and it is then that you will start learning the ways of the Universe.

Your intentions in coming to Earth and experiencing life in this 21st Century and beyond, were in part to understand that all that has gone before you, is past, and that as truth reveals itself, it will do so in miniscule portions to each and every member of your planet.

When you know and accept yourself intimately, you will draw to you those who will complement and inform you, as universal truths often come through friends and family.

When the queries arise, register them and then let them go, asking that if it be necessary for you to know the answer, then explanations will be presented at the appropriate time.

With this understanding, then all people who hold love in their hearts are to be respected and heard.

Many mysteries are being unravelled at this time, so with humility, remember you have chosen to be here on your planet and to be involved in this awakening. *With love.*

Worry

WE ARE only too pleased to discuss the ways of your world at this time and what it is that is important to you.

We see that you worry about your children and we also see that this worry distracts you from your life.

We can understand the connection that parents have with their children yet we also know that these children follow the light and guidance their parents bring to them and then they choose their own way. This is how humans evolve, yes?

Allow us to bring to you the idea that when you register what is happening with your family, and choose to stay calm within yourself, the calm and security that you emanate will reach those family members who are in need.

If we were to become agitated and anxious for our loved ones living an Earth life, then we would hardly be of light-filled assistance as is required! Consider this.

Our connection to you is strong, and our willingness to provide a peaceful and practical solution is our hearts' desire. This is part of our guardianship and is beneficial for our relationship as you allow yourself to receive from this higher guidance.

There are always answers to every query, and when the limited mind relaxes and allows the light to flow, then the process of change and transformation becomes easier for us both to engage.

Love to you, *Dear Heart*. We are filled with compassion and admiration for you at the progress you make with the building of trust and faith that is required in your world today.

There are universal changes happening with often lightening speed and we are here to be of assistance to all those who accept their place, and join with us in this transmutation. *Love always.*

Another Way

DEAR HEART, at times of great change we are always tempted to help you beyond our boundaries.

We see you struggling, yet we are aware that the progress you make is the path you have chosen, so we wait.

We are also aware of your intention to heal and grow and this often puts stress and anxiety on your human body.

Let us change more easily. Let us discuss with you ways of allowing this change you are experiencing and make it into a relaxed and easier path.

Firstly, let us remind you that you are moving through a passage of surrender that has not been experienced on your planet before this time.

The extreme manner of this powerful energy has the purpose of balancing aspects of your world that have hitherto been neglected.

With this in mind, relax and allow the peace and serenity to flow easily through you, so as to gradually strengthen and sustain you, and in this way your healing process will be enriched.

We suggest making a decision that this is how you wish to proceed.

Then allow the loving energies around you full dominion and in doing so, from the depths of your being, surrender to this masterful presence with all the personal power and strength that you can muster.

Do whatever needs to be done to stay aware that the process you are normally conditioned to experiencing has changed, and that now you are in our hands.

This is the *Way of the God/Goddess.*

Shifting the Fear

DEAR HEART we come to this page and surround you as you read these words to share our deep and abiding love for you.

May we say how brave we consider those who have chosen to experience this Earth life. You have our deepest respect and we are always of service to you whenever you call.

Often the mysteries of the Universe that flow around you are disruptive to your conditioned way of living. The easiest way to live with change is to allow its process without resistance and to relax so as not to cause undue discomfort to yourself and others.

Creative pursuits have a way of assisting at these times and as you become absorbed with your passion, the mind has time to relax and spaces between thoughts are filled by wisdom.

Exercise and sport are also beneficial in assisting with the movement needed to shift aside old boundaries and resistances and so encouraging your creative spirit to express itself.

May we say how delighted we are to be with you, reminding you of our presence in your life, and assisting you in shifting the fear of love.

Breathe Deeply

HOORAH! You see how powerful you feel when you use your breath to balance yourself.

Your own breath is your secret weapon against anxiety and stress and has the ability to relax and calm you faster than any pill or potion.

Your breath is your own powerful spirit, that when used to bring composure to your brain and body, then has the ability to supply all parts of your being with the oxygen it needs to correct itself.

Deep breathing draws in healing sustenance and love, which supplies vitality to your life blood. With this in mind your intention then is to slowly and consciously breathe in and out so as to replenish and create wellness within.

When you feel as though the world is tumbling around you, *breathe deeply* and oxygenate all the cells in your body till they refill and respond. When this oxygen is distributed well you are then able to intuit your next step.

When the brain and the body are starved of this life saving breath they are inclined to falter and you may find yourself manifesting illness and pain.

Breathing with the intention of supplying oxygen and life to every cell in your body has the ability to prevent this.

There are many books written specifically on this subject of the breath, explaining in detail the effectiveness of the different ways of breathing and how beneficial this practice is for the life of the human.

We are showing you a direction, *Dear Heart*, and we are so pleased that you have responded enthusiastically. We suggest you continue this practice of breathing and stretching.

We salute you in your bravery and we wish to say how we love sending you our most heartfelt wishes for peace and calm. *Be loved.*

Romance

WE COME together again with you, *Dear Heart,* to be of assistance in bringing our valued messages of truth. We are happy and pleased that today we suggest speaking about romancing the world.

We see the alertness within you. Romance!

Yes, we wish to discuss the notion of romance in your world today, as there is more than one concept of this word and the meanings vary.

Your idea of romance is to feel beauty and tenderness within and to respond and delight in these feelings.

We would love to expand this sentiment of romance by suggesting you look at nature, as well as all that you perceive as inanimate objects, and replace the filter over your vision, by seeing everything and everyone with romantic eyes. We would love to play with this word a little and show you ways of viewing your world romantically, as you have the ability to change life around you, bringing a smile to your heart and soul.

To read a romantic book is to resonate with the characters and to live with them and their story.

Why not create your own story and with a change of perception see life around you with a rosy glow? This then ignites the warm and loving fires within, and changes your outlook on what it is you see.

Using the energy of romance in the way we have described, presents the panorama of life as fascinating, exciting, mysterious and welcoming.

Dear Heart, you have the power to design new pathways in your brain, and so your personality will develop its own secrets of loving tenderness and present a confident sense of well-being in your world.

Romance has a way of softening the edges of life, so why not consciously call on this energy and recreate your internal vision of the future?

Mastering Your Mind

DEAR HEART, to this day you have created a story in which you have played your role with others. Parts of this story are pleasant and memorable and other parts now require you to override old patterns of reaction and recreate a new way of being.

Be comfortable with who you are at this moment, then choose to see those parts of your responses in your personality that you would prefer to change. This is a conscious plan to *master your thinking patterns* and will bring a peaceful validity to your personal truth.

You have learned well from those around you, and having made the decision to unveil your authenticity, you are now becoming acutely conscious of those ideas or thoughts that will impede your forward progress. The decision to *master your mind* and delve within to bring your own personal uniqueness to light will greatly enhance your soul and spirit.

Your individual essence with its unique qualities is your own mysterious secret.

Everyone has this opportunity to reveal their truth and in honouring themselves this way, to heave a sigh of relief, as part of your reason for being is to learn more of who you are and why you are here.

As you progress in this discovery you will experience peaceful and often euphoric sensations. Irrelevant information becomes a memory and your focus deepens on the intimacy within and the awareness of yourself as lightness and joy.

As the realisations intensify, you will discover how beauty and love are an intricate part of the fabric of your being. Some will require time in digesting this information.

To have conquered old fears and set upon the journey of *mastering your mind* to include love and joy, you will learn to trust yourself and feel the freedom of your own personal power. This will call your own guardians and guides who will support and love you with all the strength you will require to enhance a happy life.

Allow a New Way

RELAXING INTO your truth will bring surprises as it will seem as though all of a sudden all the worries and troubles that you have carried for so long are lifted, and your vision becomes clear.

The mind is so powerful that when decisions are made about aspects of your life you wish healed, magic happens.

You are aware, *Dear Heart*, of how much you are all loved by us. We are privileged to be able to come and write with you and support you in this way. Our presence in your life will bring a deeper sense of security, if you will remember that we are all here for you and willing to assist.

It takes practice to let go of the old ways of arranging your life with your mind. We are aware of this as many have been on a circuit of thinking and planning all their lives, so the idea of letting us in to help may seem strange.

We use the term 'us' so as to describe a healing and helpful energy. The truth is as you are a being encapsulated in a body, we are beings that are not.

We are all surrounded by light, love and life and it is this realisation that will allow you to let go of all your problems, ask us to help you, then relax into the peace that is provided for all of us. Once you are aware of this truth, why would you want to resist?

The mind wants to hang on. The mind that has controlled for so long does not want to relinquish its power. Yet even as you are reading this you know that in times of deep silence and beauty, there is much more to your being than the mind. This realisation then usually sets the quest for a higher path and it is here we are delighted to join with you.

Every word we have written with you is the truth, *Dear Heart.* Should you be willing to allow yourself to *feel* your way through your life, you will so easily shift your subconscious to surrender and find the peace and security this provides. We are supportive of you always, whatever path you take, and reach out with love to all.

Magical Child

DEAR HEART, we would like to revisit your magical child with you.

Prepare yourself for an adventure.

Turn, and walk backward through the years to the time you were born. All characters and experiences fall away and your path is clear to return to that moment. You gaze at yourself as a child, becoming immersed in your innocence and purity.

As a newborn you have just arrived in this world from a place of pure love and light and so vibrate brightness, beauty and hope.

As you watch this miracle baby, you see with wonder and tenderness, and are reminded of the truth of your own divine presence. You lean over and whisper:

'I am sorry I forgot how beautiful you are. I apologise to you for not having remembered sooner. I have been distracted by the story I have created with all its characters and forgot the truth of who I am in the process. Will you forgive me?'

Your infant responds to you by touching your heart with a tiny hand and you feel the return of pure love and joy.

Reaching out you gently enfold your magical child in your arms and return through the years to this day.

This babe in arms feels full of vitality, promise and hope, smiling, gurgling and touching your heart as you blend.

All the past with the old stories falls away. You have found your child, the essence of yourself brimming with wisdom and love.

Your little one wriggles in your arms, wrapping tiny fingers around yours and says,

'Let's begin again!'

GLOSSARY OF TERMS:

Being: Our essential nature in a state of existence. A human, being.

Creator: The Original Source of all creation that acted to bring the entire Universe into being.

Essence: The intrinsic purity of our complete and fundamental nature, as made perfect by our Creator.

God/Goddess: Eternal, spiritual and transcendent – creator of all and infinite in all attributes.

God, Goddess, All That Is: The pure and original source of all light and love balanced in all forms, and includes all universes, all realms, all kingdoms, all planets and all beings; spirit and human.

Grace: Grace is a gift we ask the Highest Light to grant us. It comes as subtle feelings of courage, strength, clarity, loving guidance and much more. This divine gift is given to man to assist with spiritual rebirth.

Great Spirit: An Amerindian acknowledgement of the fathers and mothers of the Universe who watch over all nations.

Guardians and Guides: We are not alone. We are surrounded by our spirit-family at all times. When we establish a respectful relationship with this family, we acknowledge their mission to assist us in the living of life.

Healing Realms: All assistance is given from the healing realms of the cosmos, to those who gratefully ask and receive.

Healing Self: An intention made to restore balance and order by activating the curative powers within, through our mind, body, soul and spirit.

Higher Self: A contactable part of our self that resides beyond the ego mind, with an uninterrupted connection to the Highest Light.

Highest Light: An eternal, infinite and illuminating presence that loves and provides for us always.

Joy: A deep feeling or condition that brings happiness, love, comfort and contentment.

Light: As sparks of the Original Light, we chose to descend and live the life that was created for us. When we are troubled and in need and wish to become more cheerful and lively, we call to the Highest Light to assist us, as was the original plan and agreement.

Meditate: An act of breathing into an inner stillness, so as to shift our consciousness to peaceful contemplation and reflection. It is here we learn to communicate with our Higher Self.

Original Light: The presence of the origin, or the beginning of all Light.

Quintessence: Within these pages, this word is referred to as the most concentrated form of Love.

Soul: A sacred part of us residing in the innermost centre of our being and that survives the body after death.

Spirit: Our personal spirit is as a flame of light within us. When ignited and nourished this dynamic influence powerfully animates the body of living things, and assists us to recognize our spiritual self. The intangible part of us, that grows like a flame when ignited.

Unconditional Love: The energies of mercy, compassion and acceptance, that are always available to us, without condition or limitation.

Wisdom: Accumulated knowledge and enlightenment that produces profound wisdom.

If you've enjoyed reading

With Love From Joy

Share the magic and

Let your friends know.

Books can be purchased through Amazon.com

Moya Love is available for personal signings

at your bookshop.

Moya Love lives in Perth, Western Australia

E: moyalove@outlook.com